# Jihad
# vs.
# Terrorism

MULTIMEDIA VERA
INTERNATIONAL

# JIHAD
# VS.
# TERRORISM

DR. MAHER HATHOUT
EDITED BY MS. SAMER HATHOUT

ISBN  1-881504-54-9 (Paperback)

Cover Design by Tarik Trad
Images: Copyright © 2002 Photodisc


To order directly from the distributor,
fax request to or write to:
Dawn Books, LLC
556 S. Fair Oaks Ave. #310
Pasadena, CA   91105
(626) 796-3041
dawnbooksllc@juno.com

*"As for such [of the unbelievers] as do not fight against you on account of [your] faith, and neither drive you forth from your homelands, God does not forbid you to show them kindness and to behave towards them with full equity: for, verily, God loves those who act equitably."* (60:8)

# **Dedication**

To
my wife
&
to the soul
of my mother.

# Acknowledgments

The information contained in this booklet comes from various persons and readings. I am grateful to many persons for their assistance. Dr. M. Fathi Osman – an eminent scholar of Islamic history who has taught in myriad prestigious institutions including Al-Azhar University of Egypt, Princeton University in the United States, as well as institutions in Algeria and Saudi Arabia – allowed me to use excerpts from his booklet on *jihad*. My brother, Dr. Hassan Hathout, an international ethicist and highly-reputed author and lecturer on Islam, contributed to the section on the ethics of war. Dr. Aslam Abdullah, editor in chief of *The Minaret*, compiled the Quranic verses and Mr. Abdelhamid Youness, previous chairperson of the Islamic Center of Southern California, classified and explained the verses according to their context. Mr. Usman Qamar provided the Biblical research, which is imperative for a balanced approach to scriptural texts. I also thank Ms. Nadia Ameri for her hard work and editorial assistance and Ms. Edina Lekovic for her revisions and proofreading.

Maher M. Hathout, M.D.
Chairman of Multimedia Vera International
Senior Advisor of the Muslim Public Affairs Council
Spokesperson for the Islamic Center of Southern California

# Contents

# Preface

The recent tragic events in New York City and Washington, DC highlight a profound need to understand the concept of *jihad*, one that has largely been misrepresented. Misinformation and misperceptions create fear and prejudice.

Therefore, it is imperative for every free mind to acquire accurate information. Within American pluralism, Muslims are the most misunderstood group.

They have yet to have a fair chance to tell the world their side of the story. They have yet to have an opportunity to explain their way of life, their ideas and ideals in a comprehensive way to other constituents of American society.

It is our duty to offer a lucid explanation and brief commentary on the concept of *jihad*. Simultaneously, we hope to engage in an intellectual dialogue with inquisitive minds about Islam at large.

The term *"jihad"* has become quite familiar. It has been inaccurately translated as "holy war," something that is alien to Islam and its literature. However, it is this meaning that has been used by the media, policy makers and even by some Muslims.

Ironically, United States policy makers use the term in both a positive and a negative sense, depending on who is being referred to: negative references refer to Iran, Iraq, Lebanon, and Palestine; positive ones refer to the Afghan *mujahideen* (freedom fighters) of the 1980's and 1990's. Therefore, it is incumbent upon us to accurately explain the concept of *jihad* and to eliminate the bias and prejudice that go hand in hand with misinformation.

# *Jihad*

Ironically, anyone may talk about it, explain it or even declare it. This chaotic approach to such a noble concept has accelerated since the tragic events of September 11, 2001. However, the confusion predates the tragedy by many years. We blame the media, special interest lobbies, politicians as well as extremists. While there is no doubt that all of these groups contributed to the misunderstanding, the main responsibility falls on our shoulders; "the mainstream" Muslim men and women who see their religion as a dynamic force to deliver humanity from the darkness of ignorance and oppression to the light of justice, mercy, peace, dignity and liberty for all human beings.

We are the ones who should reclaim our right to define our religion, according to the Quran and the teachings of Prophet Muhammad (peace be upon him), and not leave it to the pundits of sensationalist media or the extremists (be they Muslims or non-Muslims).

We are the ones who should let others know what *jihad* is and what it is not. It is not a holy war. This characterization is Crusade-coinage imposed so repeatedly that even some Muslims adopted the same false terminology. This happens despite the fact that the only thing holy in Islam is God. In reality, fighting was described in the Quran as something that is hated.

*"Fighting is ordained for you, even though it be hateful to you; but it may well be that you hate a thing the while it is good for you, and it may well be that you love a thing the while it is bad for you: and God knows, whereas you do not know."* (2:216)

The word *jihad* has a root verb: *jahada*, which in Arabic means exerting maximum effort or striving. The theological connotation is striving for betterment. Its major form is the struggle within oneself for self-improvement, elevation, purification and getting closer to God.

Another form is intellectual *jihad*, where the truth is offered to the hearts and minds of people through intellectual debate, wisdom, and dialogue, exposing the facts in the Quran in a clear and convincing way.

Related to that is the concept of *ijtihad*, which is exerting maximum effort to derive solutions and rulings from the Quran and the teachings of Prophet Muhammad, to be implemented in different and dynamically changing contexts. Another form of *jihad* is using economic power to uplift the condition of the downtrodden and to finance the struggle for justice and liberation. Last, but not least, of the forms of *jihad* is the physical form, where people actually fight against oppression. The principals of that form are stipulated clearly in the Quran and teachings of Prophet Muhammad:

1. Fighting is only to defend against those oppressors who attack Muslims to force them to convert away from their religion or to drive them out of their homes. *"As for such [of the unbelievers] as do not fight against you on account of [your] faith, and neither drive you forth from your homelands, God does not forbid you to show them kindness and to behave towards them with full equity: for, verily, God loves those who act equitably."* (60:8)

**18**

2. Fighting is limited to the combatants. *"Fight those who fight against you, and do not transgress (as the fighting is limited to combatants)."* (2:190)

3. The Prophet commanded that the life of civilians, foliage, livestock, clergy and places of worship are to be protected.

4. If the enemy inclines to peace, peace should be accepted, even at the risk of possible deception by the enemy: *"But if they incline to peace, incline thou to it as well, and place thy trust in God; verily He alone is all-hearing, all-knowing. And should they seek but to deceive thee [by their show of peace] – behold, God is enough for thee."* (8:61-62)

5. If these are the bases of war and peace, there are also rules of engagement that are applicable in the battlefield. The rules of bravery, steadfastness and resilience are all required in fighting to achieve victory. *"O you who have attained to faith: When you meet in battle those who are bent on denying the truth, advancing in great force, do not turn your back on them for whoever on that day turns his back to them– unless it be in battle maneuver, or in an endeavor to join another troop [of the believers] – shall indeed have earned the burden of God's condemnation, and his goal shall be hell: and how vile a journey's end."* (8:15-16)

6. The dignity and sustenance of the prisoners of war should be guaranteed. *"And who give food – however great be their own want for it – unto the needy, and the orphan, and the captive of war [saying in their hearts,] 'We feed you for the sake of God alone. We desire no recompense from you, nor thanks.'"* (76:9-10)

It is obvious that the concept of *jihad* is too comprehensive to be reduced simply to "war" even if described erroneously as holy.

*Jihad* is the human endeavor of striving to improve the individual and the society and to bring life closer to the divine model.

It is clear then that the word *jihad* is an Islamic-Arabic term that has been incorrectly translated and largely misunderstood. The word has been twisted in order to give the impression that Islam and Muslims are inclined towards violence; that they have a dark side. This understanding would lead people to conclude that, inherently, Muslims cannot be active participants in world peace. As mentioned before, there is no equivalent to the term "holy war" in Islamic terminology. There is no mention of "holy war" in either the Quran or *hadith* (teachings of Prophet Muhammad), which are the primary sources of Islamic teachings.

# A Justified *Jihad*

"Holy war" gives the impression that *jihad* aims to declare war against non-Muslims all over the world in order to impose Islam as a faith or as a political system by force. Such an understanding, or misunderstanding, ignores the Arabic language, the Islamic sources and the historical practice of Muslims. *Jihad* means striving to the utmost. Islam declares that the only legitimate struggle is to defend human rights – including personal freedom and freedom of faith – and is a proper form of *jihad*:

*"Permission (to fight) is given to those against whom war is being wrongfully waged – and verily, God has indeed the power to succor them – those who have been driven from their homelands against all right for no other reason than their saying, 'Our Sustainer is God!'"* (22:39-40)

*"And how could you refuse to fight in the cause of God and the utterly helpless men and women and children who are crying: 'O our Sustainer! Lead us forth [to freedom] out of this land whose people are oppressors...'"* (4:75)

# Ethics of War in Islam

In his article about ethics of war in Islam, Dr. Hassan Hathout referred to several teachings and events that will form the ethical standards that Muslim combatants ought to observe.

### Personal Behavior of the Troops

Islam places great emphasis on the personal behavior of Muslim soldiers. In war and in peace, the instructions of Islam are to be observed. Whatever is prohibited during peace is also prohibited in war. War is no excuse to be lenient with one's values. Prophet Muhammad said: "Beware of the prayer (to God) of the oppressed ... for there is no barrier between it and God even if he (the oppressed) was a non-believer." Therefore, a true believer will make every effort not to be an oppressive power.

### Fighting Norms

As mentioned previously, fighting should be directed only against fighting troops, and not against civilians. Thus, the Quran says: *"Fight in the cause of God those who fight you... and do not transgress..."* (2:190)

Prophet Muhammad's instructions to Muslim commanders in chief were: "Fight in the cause of God. Fight the combatants who deny God. Do not be embittered. Do not be treacherous. Do not mutilate. Do no kill children or those in convents."

Abu Bakr, the first caliph (head of an Islamic state), instructed Usama, the Muslim commander in chief who led the campaign
on Syria: "Do not betray or be treacherous or vindictive. Do not
mutilate. Do not kill the children, the aged or the women. Do not
cut or burn palm trees or fruit trees. Don't slay a sheep, a cow or
camel except for your food. And you will come across people
who confine themselves to worship in hermitages... Leave them
alone to what they devoted themselves for."

Abu Bakr also instructed Yazid ibn Abi Sufian: "I give you ten
commandments: don't kill a woman or a child or an old person,
and don't cut trees or ruin dwellings or slay a sheep but for food.
Don't burn palm trees or drown them. And don't be spiteful or
unjust."

## Maintain Justice and Avoid Blind Retaliation

The atrocities of the enemy are not justification for blind retal-
iation or unjust practices on the part of Muslims. The Muslim
army is not allowed to destroy civil facilities or disrupt public
amenities. The Quran says:

*"O you who have attained to faith! Be ever steadfast in your
devotion to God, bearing witness to the truth in all equity; and
never let hatred of anyone lead you into the sin of deviating from
justice. Be just: this is closest to being God-conscious. And remain
conscious of God: verily, God is aware of all that you do."* (5:8)

## Prisoners of War

Islam forbids Muslims to mistreat prisoners of war and deny
them food, shelter and other essentials of life. It adopts an attitude
of mercy and caring for the captured enemy. It was customary for
the captives to work for their food and livelihood during their cap-
tivity. The Quran made it a charity to feed prisoners saying:

**24**

*"The believers perform their vows and they fear a day whose evil flies far and wide. And they, though they hold it dear, give sustenance to the indigent, the orphan and the captive... (saying) we feed you for the sake of God alone: no reward do we desire from you, nor thanks."* (76:7-9)

Prophet Muhammad instructed his companions to treat prisoners with more than just decency. "It is my recommendation that you be good to the captives," he told his companions.

The Prophet customarily instructed his followers to collect whatever food there was and send it to the prisoners. When the members of Quraiza, a tribe that was fighting against the Muslims, were captured, loads of dates were regularly carried to them with the Prophet's instructions to shelter them from the summer sun and provide them with water to drink.

According to Islamic law, a prisoner of war became the prisoner of the state, not his captor as was the custom of the time. The head of state has the ultimate option, as he or she sees fit, of granting freedom or setting bail for the prisoner to attain freedom. Among those to whom the Prophet granted freedom was a poet called Abu-Azza who said: "I have five daughters who have no one to support them, so give me away to them as a charity and I promise never to fight you or help your enemies." He was freed for a compensation, which the Prophet later returned to him.

Umama ibn Athal was set free and subsequently converted to Islam saying to the Prophet: "There was a time when your face was the most hated face to me... and there comes a day when it is the most loved."

Sometimes captives were exchanged for Muslim captives in enemy hands. Another acceptable ransom that was quite often carried out was to teach ten Muslim children how to read and write, which testifies to the importance that Islam gave to education in the illiterate society of Arabia. Some people were set free upon their word of honor not to fight again and were advised to keep their promise and not be ordered by their tribes to go into battle again.

## Medical Care for Prisoners of War

In almost every battle fought by Muslims, nursing and medical aid was given top priority. Muslim women served as doctors and nurses to treat wounded soldiers.

Later, Muslim rulers employed Christian and Jewish doctors and many of them were court and personal physicians to caliphs. They were given encouragement and facilities to pursue their professions in full freedom.

Medical help was a right to all people regardless of religion or creed. This right was also extended to the enemy forces who needed it. For instance, during the Crusades, Saladin sent his medical advisors to help his opponent, Richard Lion Heart of England who was seriously ill. Saladin personally supervised Richard's treatment until he became well.

On the contrary, when the Crusaders entered Jerusalem on July 15, 1099, they slaughtered 70,000 Muslims, including women, children, and elderly people. They broke children's skulls by knocking them against the walls, threw babies from roof tops, roasted men over fires and cut women's bellies to see if they had swallowed gold. (Draper, *History of Intellectual Development of Europe*, Vol. 2, p. 77)

Islam decrees protection for the captives and the wounded. The believers are praised in the Quran as: "they offer food – dear as it is – to the needy, orphan or captive, (saying) we feed you for the sake of God without seeking any reward or gratitude from you." (76:8-9)

The Prophet said to his companions: "I entrust the captives to your charity." And they did, even giving them priority over themselves in the best of the food they shared. Whatever the feeling of the caregiver is, he must hold to the one and only duty of protecting life and treating the casualties of war. Whatever the behavior of the enemy, the Muslim care provider shall not change his behavior. God made it clear in the Quran: "*Let not the wrong doing of others sway you into injustice.*" (5:8)

Medical practitioners shall not permit its technical, scientific or other resources to be utilized for any sort of harm or destruction or infliction upon persons of physical, psychological, moral or other damage, regardless of political or military considerations. The Muslim doctor is obliged to offer treatment to all patients, whether they are allies or enemies.

## Against Combatants Only

This point that has been mentioned before as a rule now has to be re-emphasized as a part of ethics. *Jihad*, as a legitimate struggle against aggression, is restricted to resisting those who practice the aggression, and should not result in indiscriminate bloodshed.

The Quran stresses: "*And fight in God's cause against those who initially wage war against you, but do not commit aggression for, verily, God does not love aggressors... Thus if anyone commits aggression against you, attack him just as he attacked you – but remain conscious of God, and know that God is with those who are conscious of Him.*" (2:190, 194)

The wounded should not face any more pressure or harm, and Muslims should leave them in the care of their own forces, or provide them with medical care if they keep them as prisoners of war. The human needs of such people ought to be fulfilled (see 76:8) and they must feel secure physically and morally until they are set free and returned safely to their homes when the war comes to an end. (see 47:4)

The Muslim army was instructed by the Prophet and early Caliphs to avoid any violation of these rules or any unethical practice in war.

One who seeks shelter with Muslims has to be protected. An explanation of the message of Islam and the reason for the hostilities is offered to such a person without any pressure to accept the message. Then the shelter-seeker may enjoy security in Muslim lands or return home safely, even if there is still a possibility that he/she may turn against the Muslims. The Quran clearly states: *"And if any of those who ascribe divinity to aught beside God seeks your protection, grant him/her protection, so that he/she might (be able to) know about the message of God, and thereupon convey him/her to wherever one can feel secure."* (9:6)

Through any confrontation, Muslims adhere to the Quranic principle: *"It may well be that God will bring about (mutual) affection between you (O believers) and some of those whom you (now) face as enemies: for God is all-powerful and God is much forgiving and gracious."* (60:7)

# Let There be Peace

It is significant that one of God's names in the Quran is "The Whole Peace" or "The Source of Peace" (59:23) and that the Quran calls the Heavens and Paradise "the abode of peace."

*"And know that God invites humankind unto the abode of peace." (10:25)*

*"Theirs (those who take God's message to heart) shall be an abode of peace with their Lord."* (6:127)

In the Heavens, peace will be the greeting: *"And the angels will come unto them from every gate, saying: Peace be upon you."* (13:23-24)

*"On the Day when they meet Him, their greeting will be: Peace."* (33:44, see 10:10, 14:23, 16:32, 39:73, 50:34, 56:26)

The word Islam is derived from the Arabic word for peace, *"salam."* Just as peace is the root of the word Islam, it is also the root of its message.

*"O you who have attained to faith! Surrender yourselves wholly unto God, and follow not Satan's footsteps, for, verily, he is your open foe."* (2:208) *"Now there has come unto you from God a light, and a clear divine writ, through which God shows unto all who seek His goodly acceptance the paths leading to salvation."* (5:15-16)

Peace is customarily wished upon others by Muslims through the greeting of *"Assalamu Alaikum"* which means peace be unto you. Muslims are taught by the Quran to *"develop cooperation for furthering virtue and God-consciousness, and to avoid all that may further evil and enmity."* (5:2)

The Quran directly advises Muslims to combat temptations towards arrogance, greed and hostility with self-control and goodness. This demands finding peaceful ways for conflict resolution: *"...but since good and evil cannot be equal, repel evil with something that is better: and notice how someone who is separated from you because of enmity will become a bosom friend. Yet only those who have self-control will attain it; only the very luckiest will achieve it."* (41:34-35)

*"Those shall receive a multiplied reward for having been patient and self-controlling, and having repelled evil with good... and whenever they heard frivolous talk, they turned away from it saying: 'Unto us shall be accounted our deeds and unto you your deeds. Peace be upon you; and we don't like to be involved [in futile argument] with those who lack knowledge and self-control."* (28:54-55)

# A Divine Approach to Justice

As was noted by Dr. Fathi Osman, with the emergence of the Quran in the 7th century, Arabia was introduced to comprehensive changes in its legal system. In pre-Islamic times, settlement of disputes was sought through tribal chiefs that acted as judge and jury. Islam promoted the emergence and usage of state laws and courts. Thus, not only did the Quran advocate peace, it provided a comprehensive system designed to achieve it. Naturally, the internal peace of a nation is supported by peaceful coexistence with its neighbors in the global community. With this in mind, the Quran also provided guidelines for dealing with international disputes. Peaceful means to settle quarrels and achieve reconciliation, including direct negotiation, universal mediation, arbitration and judicial law must be pursued. The following verse provides a course of action a non-partisan mediator should follow in case of war or in case one party attacks another.

*"...Make peace between them (the two fighting groups); but if one of the two goes on committing aggression against the other, fight against the one that commits aggression until it reverts to God's commandments."* (49:9)

If a party uses force and commits aggression, non-partisan forces should confront them until they agree to abide by law and order. It is imperative to note that after aggression has ceased, the Quran requires that justice be observed in settling the issues involved, without doing injustice to either of the parties involved. Justice is an essential component of peace, as peace cannot exist without justice. Furthermore, the Quran recognizes that any unjust settlement can fuel another war.

*"And if they revert, make peace between them with justice, and deal equitably (with both groups): for verily God loves those who act equitably."* (49:9)

World courts dealing with human rights and international violations are essential for handling internal and external disputes peacefully, without using force towards any party that suffers from injustice. Islam inspires and condones such a procedure. Many instances in Islamic history demonstrated this approach. For example, when Caliph Umar ibn Abdul Aziz (717-720 A.D.) received a complaint from the people of Samarqand that the Muslim army violated an agreement and occupied their city, he ordered an inquiry into the case by the supreme judge. The supreme judge, in turn, ordered the Muslim army to withdraw.

The devastating disasters of war resulting from technological advances, and the dreadful experiences of recent wars among Muslim countries (e.g. Iraq and Iran, Libya and Chad, Iraq and the Gulf countries) should lead to stronger initiative in establishing and maintaining an international justice tribunal.

# Human Dignity

The Quran states the God has conferred dignity on all the Children of Adam, whatever their ethnicities and beliefs may be:

*"We have honored the children of Adam; provided them with transport on land and sea; given them for sustenance things good and pure; and conferred on them special favors above a great part of our creation."* (17:70)

This verse indicates the right of all people to migrate freely and the right of their pursuit of happiness regardless of race, color or creed. Human dignity has a wider concept than human rights, as dignity comprises the enjoyment of rights and the fulfillment of duties side by side. God granted dignity to humankind since our inception. Thus, the appreciation of human dignity is integral to the Muslim's belief system to a degree that cannot be rivaled by philosophical ideas or laws.

Since human beings enjoy enormous physical, intellectual, and spiritual power in the global community, we have a greater responsibility to use our power wisely. As humanity is diverse, humanity is expected not merely to tolerate diversity; rather, we are to respect diversity and to deal with others with dignity irrespective of whether the dealings are political, economic or social.

# Religious Freedom

Freedom of religion is fundamental to Islamic principles. If religion is forced, then there is no morality involved. The Quran clearly states that Islam should not be imposed on individuals or peoples against their will:

*"Let there be no coercion in matters of faith."* (2:256)

*"If it had been your Lord's will, they would all have believed (in God's message), all those who are on earth. Will you then compel people against their will, to believe?"* (10:99)

*"...Shall we compel you to accept it when you are averse to it?"* (11:28)

Prophet Muhammad's task, as indicated in the Quran, was to let others know the message: to explain and to exhort, not to impose or force: *"And so (O Prophet), exhort them; your task is only to exhort: you cannot compel them [to believe]."* (88:21-22) *"And you can by no means force them to believe: Just remind, through this Quran, all such as may fear My warning."* (50:45)

*"But would you, perhaps, torment yourself to death with grief over them if they are not willing to believe in this message? Behold, we have willed that all beauty on earth be a means by which we put people to test, (showing) which of them are best in conduct."* (18:6-7; see also 26:3)

According to Islamic theology, to be accepted by God, an embrace of faith must be both intentional and through free will, as this is the basis for acceptance on the Day of Judgment.

# Beyond Tolerance

A main source of contention in the world is insularism – the rejection of the "other," seeing the world through tunnel vision. The vicious desire to conform the world into one form, the right form in the mind of those seeking conformity.

In Islam, human diversity is God's will, and the believers in Him must learn to live in a pluralistic world:

*"And had your Lord so willed, He could surely have made all mankind one single community, but (He willed it otherwise, and so) they continue to have differences-all of them, save those upon whom your Lord has bestowed His grace (by following His guidance on cohabiting with their differences and handling them peacefully)."* (11:118-119)

*"Unto every one of you have we appointed a law and way of life. And if God had so willed, He could surely have made you all one single community, but (He willed it otherwise in order) to test you through what He has given you. Vie, then, with one another in doing good works: Unto God you all must return; and then He will make you truly understand all that in which you were used to differ."* (5:48)

When the Quran states: *"Behold, the only (true) religion in the sight of God is Islam,"*(3:19) *"And if one goes in search of a religion other than Islam, it will never be accepted from him"* (3:85), the word "Islam" signifies the general linguistic meaning which is

**37**

"submission to God," as opposed to the specific term referring to the message of Prophet Muhammad. (see 5:3, 6:125, 39:22) Islam is a noun derived from the verb *aslama* (submit). The Quran indicates that Islam, in its general meaning, was the faith of all the prophets before Muhammad. Noah reminded his people: "*I have asked no reward whatsoever from you: my reward rests with none but God and I have been bidden to be among 'the Muslims,' (those who have submitted themselves to God)*." (10:72) The same submission to God, or Islam, has been repeatedly emphasized by Abraham and his descendants:

"*And who, unless he be weak of mind, would want to abandon Abraham's creed...when His Lord said: submit yourself unto Me (aslem), he answered: I have submitted myself unto you (aslamto) the Lord of all the worlds.*

*And this very creed did Abraham entrust his children, and (so did) Jacob: O my children! Behold, God has granted you the purest faith; so do not allow death to overtake you ere you have submitted yourselves (been Muslims) to Him.*

*Were you witnesses when death was approaching Jacob, and he said to his children: whom will you worship after I am gone?*

*They answered: We will worship your God, the God of your forefathers Abraham and Ishmael and Isaac, the One God; and to Him we, submit ourselves (are Muslims)... Say (O believers in the message of Muhammad):*

*We believe in God, and in that which has the message of Muhammad): We believe in God, and in that which has been bestowed from on high upon us, and that which has been bestowed upon Abraham and Ishmael and Isaac and Jacob and their descendants, and that which has been given to Moses and Jesus, and that which has been given to all the (other) prophets by their Lord: We make no distinction (in our belief) between any of them.*

**38**

*And it is unto him that we submit ourselves (are Muslim)."* (2:130-136, see also 3:83-85)

Moses addressed the Israelites in Egypt similarly: *"And Moses said: O my people! If you believe in God, place your trust in Him – if you, 'have truly submitted yourselves to God' (have truly been Muslims)."* (10:84) When the Queen of Sheba accepted the belief in the one God preached by Solomon, she announced, *"and (now) I have submitted myself (aslamtu), the same as Solomon did – to the Lord of all the worlds"* (27:44). The early followers of Jesus made the same statements: *"We believe in God, and bear witness (O Jesus) that we submitted ourselves to Him (have been Muslims)."* (3:52)

The Quran considers a true submission to God, "Islam," as the basic belief for all monotheists. *"You, indeed, everyone who submits oneself to God, and is a doer of good withal, shall have his/her reward with his/her Lord; and all such need have no fear, and neither, shall they grieve."* (2:112)

*"And who could be better of faith than one who submits one's whole being to God, and is a doer of good withal, and follows the creed of Abraham, who turned away from all that is false..."* (4:125)

On the other hand, a *kafir* is not as it is usually translated, an "unbeliever," or as some Western scholars put it, an "infidel." According to Arabic linguistics and the Quranic use, a *kafir* is one who denies the clear fact of God's creation and favors and rejects His message while realizing within oneself the truth that he/she is opposing in words: *"And thus they deny (yakfuroon) ungratefully God's favor,"* (16:72 see also *kafarat* in 27:40), *"and he (Solomon) said: this is some of my Lord's bounty, to test me as to whether I am grateful or ungrateful (akfur)! However, who is grateful (to God) is but grateful for one's own good; and one who is ungrate-*

**39**

*ful (kafara), (should know that), verily, my Lord is free from needs and the Most Generous in giving,"* (27:40) *"and should you try to count God's favors, you could never number them; behold, the human being is so unfair, so ungrateful (kuffar: extremely kafir)."* (14:34) *"And they rejected them (God's messages and signs) wrongfully and haughtily, even though they themselves felt certain about it,* (27:14) *behold it is not you whom they give the lie, but God's messages and (signs) do these wrongdoers reject."* (6:33)

Muslims have to coexist and cohabit with such rejecters of God's favors and messages in this world fairly and peacefully, as long as they do not turn their negative feelings into aggression. Muslims are forbidden to offend or attack people who deny faith in the one God:

*"And do not insult those who they appeal to instead of God, lest they insult God out of spite and in ignorance, as we have made to every group their own doings seen attractive; in time, unto their Lord they must return, and then He will make them (truly) understand all that they were doing."* (6:108)

In this way, self-control, fairness and kindness may open the hearts and minds to the truth in the end: *"It may well be that God will bring about (mutual) affection between you (O Believers) and some of those whom you (now) face as enemies..."* (60:7)

# Universal Cooperation

Islam declares the world a peaceful place for humanity, in which people should build on constructive relationships of friendship and cooperation, whatever the ethnic or religious differences may be: "*O humankind, we have created you from a single pair or a male and female and We have made you into nations and tribes, so that you might come to know one another (not so that you may despise one another)*." (49:13)

Muslims are taught by the Quran to be scrupulously fair with others, and to judge every case on its own merits without generalization:

"*Among the People of the Book is he who, if entrusted with a great amount of wealth, will readily pay it back; and among them there is he who if entrusted with a single silver coin, will not repay it unless you constantly stand demanding.*" (3:75)

"*The people of the Book are not alike, among them there are upright people who recite God's messages throughout the night and prostrate themselves before Him. They believe in God and the Last Day (Day of Judgment), and enjoin the doing of what is right and forbid the doing of what is wrong, and vie with one another in doing good works, and they are among the righteous. And whatever good they do, they shall never be denied the reward thereof.*" (3:113-116)

**41**

Justice is repeatedly and strictly emphasized in dealing with any individual or group: *"...and no bearer of burdens shall be made to bear another's burden."* (6:164; see also 17:15, 35:18, 39:7, 53:38)

According to the Quran, justice and kindness represent the basis of Muslims' relations with others who do not initiate hostility and fighting against Muslims: *"God forbids you not, with regard to those who fight you not for your faith nor drive you out of your homes, from dealing kindly and justly with them: For God loves those who are just."* (60:8)

*Thus, if they let you be, and do not make war on you and offer you peace, God does not allow you to cause them any harm."* (4:90)

History has proved how the Muslims' behavior secured tolerance within the Muslim state, and constructive cooperation with others. Their agreements with other countries were strictly observed and peace was secured as long as they were not violated. (see 5:1, 9:4, 16:91-96, 17:34)

Even when a hidden betrayal from another party is feared, Muslims have to act openly *"And if you have reason to fear treachery from people (with whom you have made an agreement, cast it back at them in an equitable manner, and openly)."* (8:58)

# Relations with the People of the Book

Throughout the long history of Islam, Islamic states have included many non-Muslim citizens who enjoyed respect, justice, and prosperous livelihoods. Some of them virtually dominated such professions as money exchange, medicine, and trades of jewelry, gold and silver, selling herbs and drugs, certain crafts and so on. For example, the chief of the Christian community in Baghdad was the caliph's (the head of an Islamic state) physician.

Non-Muslim officials were significantly numerous in public administrations. According to a Christian source, Michael the Syrian, the chiefs of the Jewish and Magian communities in the Abbasid times were called "kings" and their positions were hereditary. Most chiefs of Eastern Christian churches were elected, and all chiefs of non-Muslim minorities represented them before the caliphs and authorities.

A Jewish traveler in the 12th century A.D. – Rabbi Benjamin von Tudela – stated that Muslims of Baghdad called the Chief Rabbi "Sir," while the Chief Rabbi in Cairo under the Fatimids was called the "prince of princes." Rabbi Petachja Von Regensberg, who traveled twenty years later in the same century, estimated the number of Jews in Muslim countries, except North Africa. He stated that Jews in Iraq alone reached 6 million.

Religious freedom was secured and non-Muslims celebrated their festivals. Muslims participated and helped organize those festivals that were attended by the caliphs, their ministers or regional governors. Public services, including medical treatment in hospitals, were offered to both Muslims and non-Muslims.

While certain minorities chose to live in the same localities, there was no segregation with regard to living quarters. They were allowed their own judges for religious and family affairs, but they had the choice of submitting their lawsuits to the state court. The Fatimid Caliph al-Aziz (975-996 A.D.) had Christian in-laws, and appointed a Christian (Eisa ibn Nestorius) as a minister, and a Jew (Menassa) as a governor of Syria. (See Adam Mez, *Die Renaissance des Islam*, Ch. IV)

Christian and Jewish people lived in safety and were protected within the Ottomon Empire.

Different Islamic states had friendly and constructive relations with other contemporary world powers. In Muslim Spain, then known as "Andalus," Muslims and Jews cooperated in developing a glorious civilization, which was a torch of light for the whole of Europe during the Middle Ages, and both groups suffered after the fall of Muslim power there. Many official visits were exchanged between Muslims and the existing world powers, including the Byzantines, the Franks, and the Chinese. Muslims developed active commercial and cultural relations with the entire known world.

Having various origins, Muslim cities represented a wide spectrum of urban and architectural origins such as Arabian, Byzantine, Iranian and Indian. Yet they also developed their own regional styles such as Moroccan-Andalusian, Egyptian, Syrian, and Eastern. Muslim ships and caravans went throughout the world, and Muslim commercial centers, hotels, marketplaces

**44**

(*bazaars*) and mail services flourished on land and sea routes in all the known continents from West Africa to the Far East. Muslim currencies were strong and universally respected. The word "check" reveals its Arabic origin (*sakk*), as merchants from Muslim countries used money orders in universal transactions. Jews and Russians had significant roles in trade between Europe and the Muslim lands. Political relations developed between the Muslim rulers and the rulers of Volga, other Slavian areas and China.

The Muslim geographer, al-Idrisi (d. 1251 A.D.) reported that some Muslim navigators went from Lisbon across the Atlantic west then south to explore and could reach a land there. (Mez: ibid, Ch. xxix, xxix)

Having said all that, we have to admit that through the succeeding centuries, Islamic principles of internal or international justice were sometimes violated, and the Muslim forces may have been used to suppress the civilian dissidents or to annex neighboring lands for mere expansionism, but this occurred against divine law. Greedy despots have emerged in the history of every nation, Muslims nations included.

Nevertheless, the principles of Islamic justice have always been clear in divine sources since the conception of humanity, as represented in the Muslim intellectual heritage under any despot or expansionist.

People generally have the ability to exploit faith or ideology or law. However, the facts about Islam in its divine sources and main practices should always be recognized in their authenticity and purity.

Likewise, the claims to Christianity by medieval Crusaders, modern Nazis or pro-life activists who bomb abortion clinics by no means should represent the teachings of the Bible.

**45**

Thus, *jihad* in Islam is essentially a system for a legitimate struggle against aggression and oppression. "*...And if God had not enabled people to defend themselves against one another, mischief would surely overwhelm the earth.*" (2:251)

# The Misquoted Verses

After the wave of curiosity that swept the nation in the aftermath of the September 11 tragedy, and as the American people showed maturity, open mindedness and a genuine desire to know about Islam, we also saw the rise of self-proclaimed experts, with various agendas. They tried to discredit Islam and Muslims by claiming that: a) Muslims are violent, and b) That this is a result of the book they believe in, the Quran.

This effort was sometimes obviously orchestrated. On one three-hour talk show featuring a Muslim, there were more than 50 calls; most of them clearly hostile. However, what was significant was that a great number of people who quoted verses of the Quran by citing the verse and chapter number, giving the impression of a level of knowledge that cannot even be found in some Islamic Schools of Theology! Knowledge that far exceeds equivalent knowledge of the Bible. Most of these quotations were loaded with incorrect translations, or were truncated and out of context, whether the context was theological or historical. I will address the most commonly misused verses. The majority of these verses refer to violent confrontation in war. Rather than going into an exhaustive and detailed discussion about each and every one, I would rather set lines of demarcation between: the basis for war and peace in the Quran, the rules of engagement and the history behind the verses.

**Basis for war and peace:**

It has been already mentioned that:

- The base of human relations is peace. War is the bitter exception.
- War is not holy. Rather, it is a last resort that is in fact hated.
- War is fought to defend against oppressors who fight people to force them away from their faith or drive them out of their homes.
- War is limited to combatants.
- Islamic ethics are to be observed.
- Peace is to be accepted if the enemy so inclines, even at the risk of later treachery or deception.

The verses that mandate these rules have been already mentioned or will be mentioned in the upcoming pages. They are permanently binding to all Muslims at all times and under any circumstances.

**Rules of engagement:**

When war is already imposed and within the limits of the battlefield, Muslims are to be patient, confident, resilient, and must fight with courage and determination. For example:

*"And kill them whenever you find them (in the field of war), and drive them out of the places where they drove you out (counter attack)."* (2:191)

*"O you who have attained to faith: when you meet in battle those who are bent on denying the truth advancing in great force, do not turn your backs on them. For whoever on that day turns his back to them on such a day – unless it be in battle maneuver, or in an endeavor to gain another group (of the believers) shall indeed have earned the burden of God's condemnation, and his goal shall be hell: and how vile a journey's end."* (8:15-16)

**48**

Clearly, these verses are applicable in the heat of battle and against an aggressive combating force.

## Verses limited to a certain historical situation:

These verses were applicable to a particular situation or if, hypothetically, the same situation was to be repeated. Several examples can be found in the following verses:

*"And fight in the way of God against those who fight against you, but begin not aggression. Verily God loves not the aggressors. And kill them wherever you find them, and drive them out of the places where they drove you out, for igniting the fire of persecution is worse than killing. And fight them not by the sacred mosque unless they fight against you there, but if they attack you there, then slay them. Such is the recompense of those who deny the truth. But if they desist, surely God is forgiving, merciful. And fight them until persecution is no more and the religion is for God, but if they desist, then let there be no hostility except against the wrongdoers."* (2:190-193)

Historically, fighting back against aggressors was prohibited during the thirteen years of the Meccan period. After the migration to Medina and the establishment of the Islamic state, Muslims were concerned with how to defend themselves against aggression from their enemies.

The aforementioned verses were revealed to enable them to protect the newly formed state by fighting in self-defense against those who fought them. However, the Quran clearly prohibits aggression. The verses explain that fighting is only for self-defense. Thus, a Muslim cannot commit aggression and kill innocent men, women, children, the sick, the elderly, monks, priests, or those who do not wish to fight. A Muslim is also mandated not to destroy plant life or livestock.

*"Fighting is ordained for you though it is hateful unto you, but it may happen that you hate a thing that is good for you. And it may happen that you love a thing that is bad for you. God knows and ye know not."* (2:216)

This verse addresses the need for Muslims of that time to answer a draft. The Quran highlights the fact that the Muslims hated fighting. Yet, the newly formed Islamic state needed to implement a defense force to be prepared in case of aggression.

*"O you who have attained to faith! Do not take for your bosom-friends people who are not of your kind. They spare no effort to corrupt you; they would love to see you in distress. Vehement hatred has already come into the open from out of their mouths, but what their hearts conceal is yet worse. We have indeed made the signs (thereof) clear unto you, if you would but use your reason."* (3:118)

The political and military situation of the time was such that the Muslims needed to be careful whom they trusted with their information. The verse does not forbid Muslims to show kindness and fairness to people who neither fought against them nor drove them out of their homes. The verse is intended to alert them during a state of war, particularly of those who show signs of hatred and resentment.

*"Those who have attained to faith fight in the cause of God, whereas those who are bent on denying the truth fight in the cause of the powers of evil. Fight, then, against those friends of Satan: verily, Satan's guile is weak indeed!"* (4:76)

This verse is related to the two preceding verses (see 4:74-75) where it was stated that those who fight for God's cause would be rewarded whether they are victorious or slain. Fighting for God's cause includes the liberation of the oppressed, meaning the helpless men and women who are yearning and praying for freedom. The believers fight for God's cause, and the disbelievers fight for the sake of their idols. An idol may be taken conceptually. For example, evil or greed may figuratively be construed as idols. The believers should put all their trust in God the Almighty and Powerful and fear not the disbelievers and their evil plans. Evil plans are always inferior to goodness.

*"O you who believe! Take not the Jews and Christians for your allies: they are but allies of one another and whoever of you allies himself with them becomes one of them. Behold, God does not guide such wrong doers."* (5:51)

"Your allies" used to translate the Arabic word *"awleya"* which actually means superior protectors. In the environment of war, Muslims who were under attack were admonished to seek their protection with God, and to keep their community aware of the danger of leaking secrets that may benefit the enemy. So this is not an absolute permanent attitude. Otherwise, it will contradict the permission of Islam to marry women of the people of the book, which is a relationship that goes far beyond friendship or alliance.

*"You will surely find that of all people, the most hostile to those who believe (in the divine writ) are the Jews and the Polytheists, and you will find the nearest of them in affection to those who believe are those who say, 'Behold, we are Christians.' That is because there are among them priests and monks and because they are not arrogant."* (5:82)

Because of the oppression under the Meccan polytheists, some Muslims migrated to Abyssinia, a Christian country. The Muslims had a chance to recite the Quran in the presence of the king, priests, and monks whose eyes overflowed with tears because they recognized something of its truth. The king granted asylum to the Muslims (see 5:83). Meanwhile in Medina, the Jews showed hostility and hatred to the Muslims. The above verse (5:82) was revealed to compare the treatment of the Muslims by the Jews and polytheists on the one hand, and the Christians on the other hand. God reprimanded the

Jews of Medina for allying themselves with polytheists over monotheists. Thus, this verse relates specifically to Christians and Jews in the context of that particular era. As a matter of fact, history has shown that, with the exception of Palestine, the Jews generally had good relations with the Muslims while Christians waged crusades against Muslims and colonized Muslim lands and peoples.

*"And fight against them until there is no more oppression and all worship is devoted to God alone. And if they desist – behold, God sees all that they do."* (8:39)

The people of Mecca persecuted Muslims for thirteen years. After the migration of Muslims to Medina and in the second year of *hijra* (migration), the Battle of Badr took place between the Muslims and the Meccans. The Muslims won the battle and were directed in this verse to continue fighting them until they end the persecution and allow freedom of religion to worship God alone. Freedom of religion is one of the most important tenants of Islam, as God says: *"There is no compulsion in religion."* (2:256)

*"Then, when the sacred months are over, slay the idolaters wherever you find them. And take them captive, and besiege them, and prepare for them each ambush, but if they repent and establish prayers and pay alms, then let them go their way. Verily, God is forgiving, merciful."* (9:5)

This verse was revealed towards the end of the revelation period and relates to a limited context. Hostilities were frozen for a three-month period during which the Arabs pledged not to wage war. Prophet Muhammad was inspired to use this period to encourage the combatants to join the Muslim ranks or, if they chose, to leave the area that was under Muslim rule; however, if they were to resume hostilities, then the Muslims would fight back until victorious. One is inspired to note that even in this context of war, the verse concludes by emphasizing the divine attributes of mercy and forgiveness. To minimize hostilities, the Quran ordered Muslims to grant asylum to anyone, even an enemy, who sought refuge. Asylum would be granted according to the customs of chivalry; the person would be told the message of the Quran but not coerced into accepting that message. Thereafter, he or she would be escorted to safety regardless of his or her religion. (9:6).

*"Fight those who believe not in God and the Last Day and do not forbid what God and his messenger have forbidden. Such persons as practice not the religion of truth, being of those who have been given the book, until they pay the exemption tax with a willing hand and have been humbled."* (9:29)

Freedom of religion is an essential aspect in an Islamic state. One of the five pillars of Islam is *zakat* (almsgiving). The People of the Book (Christians and Jews) are not obliged to pay the Islamic *zakat* that is spent by the state for social necessities and state affairs as defined in the Quran (see 9:60). But they must pay other taxes to share in the state budget. If they refuse to pay this tax to the state and rebel against the state, then it is the obligation of the state to confront them until they pay it. The same goes for Muslims; if some do not pay the *zakat*, the state must confront them until they pay it. This is what Caliph Abu Bakr did after the death of the Prophet, when some people refused to pay their *zakat*.

*"And fight against the polytheists collectively as they fight you collectively, and know that God is with those who are conscious of Him."* (9:36)

Wars against the polytheists must follow the same divine rules of fighting for God's cause.

1) Fighting in defense of self or in defense of others against those who try to drive Muslims out of their homelands.
2) Fighting in defense of freedom of religion.
3) Fighting for the freedom of the oppressed and persecuted.

53

*"O Prophet, strive against the disbelievers and the hypocrites and be firm with them, and their ultimate abode is hell, and what a miserable end."* (9:73)

This verse refers to the rebel tribes around Mecca who were rejecting any central authority and attacked the Muslims in a guerrilla war manner.

Quoting parts of any scripture without being aware of what is general and what is specific, or what is permanent versus what is pertinent to a certain historical situation is doing injustice to an intelligent understanding of the text. It is only fair to state that this reductionism is not only done by people who have an agenda to malign Islam, but by some Muslims, particularly those using Islam from an angle of anger and who wish to justify their ideologies and extremism by blurring the lines elucidated in the Quran.

# Reading Other Sacred Texts

If the Bible were to be quoted in the same manner that the Quran has been quoted, one would also come away with a distorted understanding of the Bible. If we look at it through biases and a lens of selectivity and focus solely on the issue of violence in the Bible, we will find an abundance of material.

If this material is taken out of historical context and separated from the basic essence of the message, it can be used to misguide fanatics and disfigure the face of a religion. Here are some examples:

**Judges 16:27-30**

27 Now the house was full of men and women; and all the lords of the Philistines were there; and there were upon the roof about three thousand men and women, that beheld while Samson made sport.

28 And Samson called unto the Lord, and said, O Lord God, remember me, I pray thee, and strengthen me, I pray thee, only this once, O God, that I may be at once avenged of the Philistines for my two eyes.

29 And Samson took hold of the two middle pillars upon which the house stood, and on which it was borne up, of the one with his right hand, and of the other with his left.

30 And Samson said, let me die with the Philistines. And he

bowed himself with all his might; and the house fell upon the lords, and upon all the people that were therein. So the dead whom he slew at his death were more than they that he slew in his life.

In sum, Samson, with the help of the Lord, pulls down the pillars of the Philistine house and causes his own death and that of 3000 other men and women.

### Leviticus 20:27

27. And as for man or woman in whom there proves to be a mediumistic spirit or spirit of prediction, they should be put to death without fail. They should pelt them to death with stones. Their own blood is upon them.

### Judges 15:14-16

14 And when he came unto Lehi, the Philistines shouted against him: and the Spirit of the Lord came mightily upon him, and the cords that were upon his arms became as flax that was burnt with fire, and his bands loosed from off his hands.

15 And he found a new jawbone of an ass, and put forth his hand, and took it, and slew a thousand men therewith.

16 And Samson said, with the jawbone of an ass, heaps upon heaps, with the jaw of an ass have I slain a thousand men.

To summarize, Samson slays 1,000 men with the jawbone of a donkey.

### Numbers 31:31-40

31 And Moses and Eleazar the priest did as the Lord commanded Moses.

32 And the booty, being the rest of the prey which the men of war had caught, was six hundred thousand and seventy thousand and five thousand sheep,

33 And threescore and twelve thousand beeves,

34 And threescore and one thousand asses,

35 And thirty and two thousand persons in all, of women that had not known man by lying with him.

36 And the half, which was the portion of them that went out to war, was in number three hundred thousand and seven and thirty thousand and five hundred sheep:

37 And the Lord's tribute of the sheep was six hundred and threescore and fifteen.

38 And the beeves were thirty and six thousand; of which the Lord's tribute was threescore and twelve.

39 And the asses were thirty thousand and five hundred; of which the Lord's tribute was threescore and one.

40 And the persons were sixteen thousand; of which the Lord's tribute was thirty and two persons.

In brief, 32,000 virgins are taken by the Israelites as booty. Thirty-two persons were set aside as a tribute for the Lord.

### Genesis 34:13-29

13 And the sons of Jacob answered Shechem and Hamor his father deceitfully, and said, because he had defiled, Dinah, their sister:

14 And they said unto them, We cannot do this thing, to give our sister to one that is uncircumcised; for that were a reproach unto us:

15 But in this will we consent unto you: If ye will be as we be, that every male of you be circumcised;

16 Then will we give our daughters unto you, and we will take

your daughters to us, and we will dwell with you, and we will become one people.

17 But if ye will not hearken unto us, to be circumcised; then will we take our daughter, and we will be gone.

18 And their words pleased Hamor, and Shechem Hamor's son.

19 And the young man deferred not to do the thing, because he had delight in Jacob's daughter: and he was more honorable than all the house of his father.

20 And Hamor and Shechem his son came unto the gate of their city, and communed with the men of their city, saying,

21 These men are peaceable with us; therefore let them dwell in the land, and trade therein; for the land, behold, it is large enough for them; let us take their daughters to us for wives, and let us give them our daughters.

22 Only herein will the men consent unto us for to dwell with us, to be one people, if every male among us were circumcised, as they are circumcised.

23 Shall not their cattle and their substance and every beast of theirs be ours? Only let us consent unto them, and they will dwell with us.

24 And unto Hamor and unto Shechem his son hearkened all that went out of the gate of his city; and every male was circumcised, all that went out of the gate of his city.

25 And it came to pass on the third day, when they were sore, that two of the sons of Jacob, Simeon and Levi, Dinah's brethren, took each man his sword, and came upon the city boldly, and slew all the males.

26 And they slew Hamor and Shechem his son with the edge of the sword, and took Dinah out of Shechem's house, and went out.

27 The sons of Jacob came upon the slain, and spoiled the city, because they had defiled their sister.

28 They took their sheep, and their oxen, and their asses, and that which was in the city, and that which was in the field,

29 And all their wealth, and all their little ones, and their wives took they captive, and spoiled even all that was in the house.

In this passage, the Israelites kill Hamor, his son, and all the men of their village and plunder their wealth, wives and children.

## Numbers 21:2-3

2 And Israel vowed a vow unto the Lord, and said, if thou wilt indeed deliver this people into my hand, then I will utterly destroy their cities.

3 And the Lord hearkened to the voice of Israel, and delivered up the Canaanites; and they utterly destroyed them and their cities: and he called the name of the place Hormah.

## Numbers 21:32-35

32 And Moses sent to spy out Jaazer, and they took the villages thereof, and drove out the Amorites that were there.

33 And they turned and went up by the way of Bashan: and Og the king of Bashan went out against them, he, and all his people, to the battle at Edrei.

34 And the Lord said unto Moses, Fear him not: for I have delivered him into thy hand, and all his people, and his land; and thou shalt do to him as thou didst unto Sihon king of the Amorites, which dwelt at Heshbon.

35 So they smote him, and his sons, and all his people, until there was none left him alive: and they possessed his land.

In sum, with the Lord's approval, the Israelites slay Og "... and his sons and all his people, until there was not one survivor left...."

## Numbers 25:1-9

1 And Israel abode in Shittim, and the people began to commit whoredom with the daughters of Moab.

2 And they called the people unto the sacrifices of their gods: and the people did eat, and bowed down to their gods.

3 And Israel joined himself unto Baalpeor: and the anger of the Lord was kindled against Israel.

4 And the Lord said unto Moses, Take all the heads of the people, and hang them up before the Lord against the sun, that the fierce anger of the Lord may be turned away from Israel.

5 And Moses said unto the judges of Israel, Slay ye every one his men that were joined unto Baalpeor.

6 And, behold, one of the children of Israel came and brought unto his brethren a Midianitish woman in the sight of Moses, and in the sight of all the congregation of the children of Israel, who were weeping before the door of the tabernacle of the congregation.

7 And when Phinehas, the son of Eleazar, the son of Aaron the priest, saw it, he rose up from among the congregation, and took a javelin in his hand;

8 And he went after the man of Israel into the tent, and thrust both of them through, the man of Israel, and the woman through her belly. So the plague was stayed from the children of Israel.

9 And those that died in the plague were twenty four thousand.

In short, the Lord told Moses to take all the heads of the people and hang them up before the Lord against the sun.

## Numbers 31:17-18

17 Now therefore kill every male among the little ones, and kill every woman that hath known man by lying with him.

18 But all the women children, that have not known a man by lying with him, keep alive for yourselves.

## Deuteronomy 2:31-34

31 And the Lord said unto me, Behold, I have begun to give Sihon and his land before thee: begin to possess, that thou mayest inherit his land.

32 Then Sihon came out against us, he and all his people, to fight at Jahaz.

33 And the Lord our God delivered him before us; and we smote him, and his sons, and all his people.

34 And we took all his cities at that time, and utterly destroyed the men, and the women, and the little ones, of every city, we left none to remain.

In short, the Israelites utterly destroy the men, women, and children of Sihon.

## Deuteronomy 7:1-2

1 When the Lord thy God shall bring thee into the land whither thou goest to possess it, and hath cast out many nations before thee, the Hittites, and the Girgashites, and the Amorites, and the Canaanites, and the Perizzites, and the Hivites, and the Jebusites, seven nations greater and mightier than thou;

2 And when the Lord thy God shall deliver them before thee; thou shalt smite them, and utterly destroy them; thou shalt make no covenant with them, nor show mercy unto them.

## Joshua 11:20-22

20 For it was of the Lord to harden their hearts, that they should come against Israel in battle, that he might destroy them utterly, and that they might have no favor, but that he might destroy them, as the Lord commanded Moses.

21 And at that time came Joshua, and cut off the Anakims from the mountains, from Hebron, from Debir, from Anab, and from all the mountains of Judah, and from all the mountains of Israel: Joshua destroyed them utterly with their cities.

22 There was none of the Anakims left in the land of the children of Israel: only in Gaza, in Gath, and in Ashdod, there remained.

## Judges 20:43-48

43 Thus they enclosed the Benjamites round about, and chased them, and trode them down with ease over against Gibeah toward the sun rising.

44 And there fell of Benjamin eighteen thousand men; all these were men of valor.

45 And they turned and fled toward the wilderness unto the rock of Rimmon: and they gleaned of them in the highways five thousand men; and pursued hard after them unto Gidom, and slew two thousand men of them.

46 So that all which fell that day of Benjamin were twenty and five thousand men that drew the sword; all these were men of valor.

47 But six hundred men turned and fled to the wilderness unto the rock Rimmon, and abode in the rock Rimmon four months.

48 And the men of Israel turned again upon the children of Benjamin, and smote them with the edge of the sword, as well the men of every city, as the beast, and all that came to hand: also they set on fire all the cities that they came to.

In short, the Israelites smite over 25,000 "men of valor" from amongst the Benjamites, "men and beasts and all that they found," and set their towns on fire.

### Samuel 30:17

17 And David smote them from the twilight even unto the evening of the next day: and there escaped not a man of them, save four hundred young men, which rode upon camels, and fled.

### Isaiah 13:15-18

15 Every one that is found shall be thrust through; and every one that is joined unto them shall fall by the sword.

16 Their children also shall be dashed to pieces before their eyes; their houses shall be spoiled, and their wives ravished.

17 Behold, I will stir up the Medes against them, which shall not regard silver; and as for gold, they shall not delight in it.

18 Their bows also shall dash the young men to pieces; and they shall have no pity on the fruit of the womb; their eyes shall not spare children.

## Ezekiel 9:4-7

4 And the Lord said unto him, Go through the midst of the city, through the midst of Jerusalem, and set a mark upon the foreheads of the men that sigh and that cry for all the abominations that be done in the midst thereof.

5 And to the others he said in mine hearing, Go ye after him through the city, and smite: let not your eye spare, neither have ye pity:

6 Slay utterly old and young, both maids, and little children, and women: but come not near any man upon whom is the mark; and begin at my sanctuary. Then they began at the ancient men that were before the house.

7 And he said unto them, Defile the house, and fill the courts with the slain: go ye forth. And they went forth, and slew in the city.

Basically, the Lord commands: "... slay old men outright, young men and maidens, little children and women...."

The aforementioned excerpts of the Bible are not and should not be extracted out of their context, or be stripped of their historicity in order to discredit the Bible as the light that will guide people or as a book of moral and ethical values.

# Terrorism:
# the Antithesis of *Jihad*

In spite of the difficulty of finding one comprehensive scientific definition for terrorism, yet the public perceives terrorism as a politically or ideologically motivated action that targets deliberately or at least callously, civilian non-combatants to inspire fear and to achieve certain political ends.

Under U.S. law, an "act of terrorism" means any activity that (a) involves a violent act or an act dangerous to human life that is a violation of the criminal laws of the United States or any state, or that would be a criminal violation if committed within the jurisdiction of the United States or of any state; and (b) appears to be intended to (i) intimidate or coerce a civilian population, (ii) to influence the policy of a government by intimidation or coercion; or (iii) to affect the conduct of a government by assassination or kidnapping.

Admitting the limitations of the above definition and being aware of the omittance of the whole subject of state terrorism, yet we can clearly see how far terrorism is from the noble concept of the physical form of *jihad*.

We may briefly summarize the differences in the following:
1) *Jihad* is to be launched by the recognized and established Muslim authority, as a policy of the collectivity of the Muslims, to deter aggression. Terrorism, on the other hand is committed by

individuals or clandestine groups that neither represent the majority of Muslims nor did they receive any authorization from them.

2) *Jihad* is to be declared, while acts of terrorism are born in secrecy and executed as a deadly surprise.

3) *Jihad* is limited to combatants who represent a real danger to the Muslim military, while terrorism is usually directed to the soft spots of innocent civilians in a non-discriminatory way.

4) *Jihad* is bound to the ceasing of hostility and accepting peace if the combating enemy inclines to peace, while terrorism is launched against people who are at a state of peace to start with.

Hence, any confusion between the destructive menace of terrorism and the constructive noble concept of *jihad* should never be allowed. Such a confusion is a travesty of intellect and an insult to religion.

# Conclusion

Every aspect of each Quranic mandate is aimed at nurturing an environment that will allow peace to emerge and prevail. Recognizing that humanity is flawed and will err, Islam provides a system to eradicate injustice and allow peace to flourish. In the spirit of its universal message of peace and respect for diversity, Islam's goal is not to impose itself by force or declare war against non-Muslims. Forcing Islam onto the masses contradicts the spirit of the Quran.

*Jihad* is the legitimate defense of human rights and freedom. It is restricted to cases of aggression and oppression. Should cases of aggression or oppression occur, Muslims must always fight fairly and be inclined towards peace as soon as an opportunity for a cease-fire presents itself.

*"And if they incline to peace, incline to it as well, and place your trust in God. Verily, He alone is all hearing, all knowing! And should they seek but to deceive you (by their show of peace), behold, God is enough for you."* (8:61)

Peace and justice are always superior to war for those who are conscious of God.

# A Select Bibliography

Abou El Fadl, Khaled: *The Authoritative and the Authoritarian in Islamic Discourse*, Dar Taiba.

Al-Ghazali, Muhammad: *Thurathuna al Fikri fi Mizan al Sharia wa al Aqule*, International Institute of Islamic Thought.

Al-Ghazali, Muhammad: *Mushkilat fi Tariq al Hayat al Islamiya*, Kitab al Ummah.

Al-Ghazali Muhammad: *Fiqh al Sira*, International Institute of Islamic Thought.

Al Wazeer Ben Zeyd: *Al Fardya*, The Yemenite Center of Heritage and Research.

Armstrong, Karen: *Muhammad: A Biography of the Prophet*, Harper Collins.

Arnold, Thomas: *The Spread of Islam in the World: A History of Peaceful Preaching*, Goodword Books.

Asad, Muhammad: *The Message of the Quran* , Dar al Andalus.

Dekmejian, Richard: *Islam in Revolution: Fundamentalism in the Arab World,* Syracuse University Press.

Haddad, Yvonne: *Contemporary Islam and the Challenges of History*, State University of New York.

Hathout, Hassan: *Reading the Muslim Mind*, American Trust Publications.

Howeidi, Fahmi: *Muwatinoon la Zimmiyoon*, Dar al Shorook.

*New World Translation of the Holy Scripture*s, New World Bible Translation Committee.

Kishk, Muhammad Gelal: *A Muslim Reflection on Jihad, Minorities and the Bible*, Modern Publications.

Lewis, Bernard: *The Political Language of Islam*, The University of Chicago Press.

Osman, Fathi: *Sharia in Contemporary Society*, MVI.

Osman, Fathi: *Muslim World Issues and Challenges*, MVI.

Osman, Fathi: *The Concepts of the Quran, A Topical Reading*, MVI.

Pipes, Daniel: *In the Path of God, Islam and Political Power*, Basic Books Inc.

# Verses on People of the Book

*And had your Lord willed, He would have made all humankind one single people; but (He willed it otherwise, and so) they continue to have their differences (to test them as to how they tackle them), except those upon whom your Lord has bestowed His grace (through benefiting from His guidance in resolving their differences). And to that end (of testing them) has He created them (all). But (as for those who refuse to resolve their differences rightfully and to benefit from the divine guidance), your Lord's words shall be fulfilled: "I shall assuredly fill hell with (the evil-doers from) the invisible beings and the human beings as well." (11:118-9)*

*Let there be no coercion in matters of faith; the right way has become distinct from (the way of) error. Hence, whoever rejects the powers of injustice and evil and believes in God has indeed taken hold of the most unfailing support that shall never give way, and God is All-hearing, All-knowing. (2:256)*

*Thus, if they come to you (in order to rule among them), you may either rule among them or leave them (to deal with their matter on their own); and if you let them (on their own) they cannot cause you any harm; but if you (decide to) rule among them, rule with justice; verily, God loves those who act with justice. (5:42)*

*But how is it that they ask you to be their judge, seeing that they have the Torah that contains God's rules, then thereafter they turn their backs (to it)? (5:43)*

71

*Verily, We sent down the Torah, wherein there is guidance and light, thereby the Prophets who submitted themselves to God judge among the Jewish people, and so did the people who were truly devoted to God (rabbis), and the distinctive persons, in as much as what of God's writ had been entrusted to them and they were witnesses to. Therefore, (O children of Israel) fear not people, but fear you only Me; and sell not My messages for a trifling gain; and whoever judges not according to what God has sent down, they are the stubborn deniers of the truth. And therein (in the Torah) We ordained for them a life for a life, and an eye for an eye, and a nose for a nose, and an ear for an ear, and a tooth for a tooth; and a (similar) retribution for wounds; but whosoever forgoes (this) out of generosity and magnanimity, that shall be for him(/her) an expiation (for some past wrongdoing). And whoever does not rule according to what God has sent down – they are the evildoers. (5:43-45)*

*And we sent 'Isa ibn Maryam (Jesus the son of Mary) to follow in the footsteps of those (earlier prophets), confirming the truth of the Torah that he found before him, and We gave to him the Gospel, wherein is guidance and light, confirming the truth of the Torah that he found there before him, and as a guidance and an admonition unto those who are God-conscious. And the followers of the Gospel are bidden to judge in accordance with what God has sent down therein, and they who do not judge in accordance with what God has sent down, they are truly the iniquitous. (5:46-7)*

*And to you We have sent the Book, setting forth the truth, confirming the truth of whatever remains of earlier revealed books, and watching over it; so judge between them (the People of the Book) according to what God has revealed, and follow not their whims, diverging from the truth that has come to you. To each of you We have appointed a law and a way to follow. And had God so willed, He would have made you all one single people, but (He willed it otherwise) so as to test you through what He has given you. Vie, then, with one another, in good deeds; unto God you shall return, and He will make you understand all on which you differed. (5:48)*

*And if they would but truly observe the Torah and the Gospel and what was sent down to them from their Lord, they would eat of the blessings of what is above them and what is underneath them. Some of them do reasonably behave but many of them do indeed what is wrong. (5:66)*

*Say: "O people of the Book! You have no valid ground unless you (truly) apply the Torah and the Gospel and all that was sent to you by your Lord." Yet, what has been sent to you by your Lord makes many of them react with more arrogant aggression and stubborn rejection of the truth; but you should not feel any sorrow for those who stubbornly deny the truth. (5:68)*

*Invite (all humanity) to the way of your Lord with wisdom and goodly exhortation, and argue with them in the fairest and most constructive manner; for your Lord knows best as to who strays from His path, and best knows He as to who are the right-guided. (16:125)*

*And do not argue with the people of the Book, except in the most kindly and constructive way, unless it be with those who are bent on evil doing (with whom you have to avoid any argument), and say: "We believe in what has been sent down to us, and in that which has been sent down to you; our God and your God is one; and it is to Him that we (all) submit ourselves." (29:46)*

*Say,"O People of the Book! Come unto the (basic) word which we and you both can hold, that we (together) shall worship none but the One God, and shall never associate any else with Him, nor shall we take from among us lords instead of God." And if they turn away, then say," Bear witness that we have submitted our whole-selves unto Him." (3:64)*

*We have sent to you (O Muhammad) revelation, as We sent it to Nuh (Noah) and the prophets after him; and (also) We sent inspiration to Ibrahim (Abraham), and Isma'il (Ishmael), and Is-haq (Isaac) and Ya'qub (Jacob) and their descendants (the tribes, al-Asbat); and to 'Isa (Jesus), and Ayyub (Job), and Yunus (Jonah), and Harun*

73

*(Aaron), and Sulayman (Solomon), and to Dawud (David) We gave a book of divine wisdom. About some conveyors of God's messages We have told you; about others We have not; and to Moses God spoke directly. These conveyors of God's messages who bear good tidings and warning (were sent by God), so that people might have no excuse before God after (the coming) of the conveyors of God's messages, and God is indeed All-mighty, All-wise.* (4:163-165)

*To each of you We have appointed a law and a way to follow. And had God so willed, He would have made you all one single people, but (He willed it otherwise) so as to test you through what He has given you. Vie, then, with one another, in good deeds; unto God you shall return, and He will make you understand all on which you differed.* (5:48)

*And never have We sent forth any conveyor of God's message otherwise than (with a message) in his own people's tongue, so that he might make (the truth) clear to them, then God lets go astray one that He wills, and lets be guided one that He wills (according to what each person chooses by his/her free will granted by God), and He alone is the All-mighty, All-wise.* (14:4)

*And We assuredly sent among every people a conveyor of God's message saying: "Worship God, and turn aside of the powers of evil and injustice." And then among these people were some whom God has guided, while others inevitably fell into serious erroneousness. Go, then, about the earth, and find out what was the end of those who denounced the truth as a lie.* (16:36)

*And before your time We never sent (as conveyors of Our messages) any(one) but (mortal) men to whom We sent revelation of (the truth); and if you (O people) have not realized this, ask those who have knowledge (of earlier revelations). (We sent them) with clear evidence of truth and with books of divine wisdom. And upon you We have sent down this reminder, so that you might make clear to people what is sent to them, and so that they might reflect.* (16:43-44)

*And before your time We never sent any conveyor of (Our) message except with our revelation (which he had to convey to people) that there is no deity save Me, (and that) therefore you worship Me (alone).* (21:25)

*Verily, (O you who believe in Me), this community of yours is one wholeness (umma), and I am the Lord of you all; worship, then, Me (alone).* (21:92)

*And We sent not as Our message-conveyors before you but that they ate food and went about in the market-places, for We cause you (human beings) to be a testing for one another. Will you, then, endure such a testing with patience? Your Lord is All-seeing.* (25:20)

*Yet, your Lord would never destroy towns until He sent to the principal one amidst them a conveyor of God's message, conveying our signs and messages; and never would We destroy towns except (as a result of the people's deeds) when their inhabitants are indulged in evil-doing.* (28:59)

*And (call to mind that) We took from the Prophets their solemn pledge, and from you (O Muhammad) as well as from Nuh (Noah), Ibrahim (Abraham), Musa (Moses), and 'Isa ibn Maryam (Jesus the Son of Mary) – We took from (all of) them a weighty solemn pledge, so that God might ask the truthful about their truthfulness, and grievous suffering has He readied for all who stubbornly deny the truth.* (33:7-8)

*Surely, We have sent you (O Muhammad) with the truth as a bearer of good tidings and a warning; and there never was a people who had no warner.* (35:24)

*Say: "We believe in God, and in that which has been sent down to us, and that which has been sent down to Ibrahim (Abraham) and Isma'il (Ishmael) and Is-haq (Isaac) and Ya'qub (Jacob) and their descendants (the tribes/ al-Asbat), and that which has been given to Musa (Moses) and 'Isa (Jesus) and that which has been given to all the prophets by their Lord; we make no differentiation between them (with regard to our belief in their prophethood), and it is unto Him that we submit ourselves.*  (2:136; see also 3:84)

*O you who have attained to faith! Hold fast unto your belief in God and the Conveyor of His message and in the Book. He has sent down step by step to the Conveyor of His message and the Book which He sent down before. And one who stubbornly denies God and His angels and His books and the conveyors of His messages and the Last Day has surely gone far astray.*  (4:136)

*Those who stubbornly deny God and the conveyors of His messages, and desire to make a distinction between the conveyors of His messages, saying: "We believe in one but deny the other," desiring to take a way in between; it is they who are truly (and arbitrarily) denying the truth; and We have readied for those who stubbornly deny the truth humiliating suffering. But as for those who believe in God and the conveyors of His message and make no distinction between any of them (with regard to their prophethood), We shall grant them their rewards (in full), and God is All-forgiving, Most Gracious.* (4:150-152)

*With regard to faith, He has instituted for you what He had enjoined upon Nuh (Noah), and what We have revealed to you (O Muhammad), as well as what We had enjoined upon Ibrahim (Abraham) and Musa (Moses) and Isa (Jesus): that you steadfastly uphold the faith, and do not cause divisions therein. Those who associate others with God, see what you are calling them to is beyond any acceptability on their side; God draws unto Himself one whom He wills (as He has granted every human being and free will), and guides unto Himself everyone who turns unto Him.* (42:13)

*And who could be of better faith than one who submits his (/her) whole self unto God, doing this sincerely and doing good, and follows the creed of Ibrahim (Abraham) who turned away from all that is false? And God exalted Ibrahim (Abraham) with His love.* (4:125)

*Say: "My Lord has guided me to a straight path through the ever-true faith of Ibrahim (Abraham), who turned away from all that is*

*false and who was never of those who associate others with God.*
(6:161)

*And lastly, We have sent Our revelation to you (O Muhammad, telling you:) 'Follow the creed of Abraham who turned away from all that is false and was never of those who associate others with God.'*
(16:123)

*Surely, as for those who have attained to faith (in this divine writ) and those who follow Judaism and those who turned away (from a previous faith in search for the truth) and the Christians, and the Magians, and (even) those who associate others with God: God will decide between them on Resurrection Day; and God is witness unto everything.* (22:17)